Tikkun Olam

A JEWISH APPROACH FOR REDEEMING THE
WORLD

Juan Marcos Bejarano Gutierrez

Yaron Publishing
Grand Prairie, TX

Juan Marcos Bejarano Gutierrez/Yaron Publishing
701 Forest Park Place
Grand Prairie, Texas 75052
CryptoJewishEducation.com

Book Layout ©2017 BookDesignTemplates.com

Ordering Information:
Quantity sales. Special discounts are available on quantity purchases by corporations, associations, and others. For details, contact the "Special Sales Department" at the address above.

Tikkun Olam: A Jewish View of Salvation/ Juan Marcos Bejarano Gutierrez. —1st ed.
ISBN 978-1983350429

Contents

To my sons
Eliel Nathan and Yaron Eliav

בְּטַח אֶל-יְהוָה, בְּכָל-לִבֶּךָ; וְאֶל-בִּינָתְךָ, אַל-תִּשָּׁעֵן.

"Yea, He saith: 'It is too light a thing that thou shouldest be My servant to raise up the tribes of Jacob, and to restore the offspring of Israel; I will also give thee for a light of the nations, that My salvation may be unto the end of the earth.'"
—THE PROPHET ISAIAH 49:6

CHAPTER 1

Tikkun Olam

Tikkun Olam means repairing, improving, or perfecting the world. This concept has pervaded Jewish thought throughout the ages. The actual phrase *Tikkun Olam*, however, is seldom found explicitly in Jewish sources. Nevertheless, one could argue that it remains the heart of classical Judaism.

Modern movements in Judaism often embrace their particular understanding of Tikkun Olam as the principle or ideal that the Jewish community can best embrace to contribute to the betterment of modern society. The websites for Reform Temples and Conservative synagogues almost always include a page dedicated to this idea. Now as a note to the Jewish reader, liberal Jewish movements in America have interpreted the classical concept of Tikkun Olam in light of current Jewish participation in modern politics. David Shatz highlighted this when he stated:

"American Reform Judaism, which has put most of its religious emphasis on Tikkun Olam, frequently points to Jeremiah 29:7 as a mandate for Jewish political involvement." [1]

The prophet Jeremiah states:

"And seek the peace of the city whither I have caused you to be carried away captive, and pray unto the LORD for it; for in the peace thereof shall ye have peace."[2]

---

[1] David Shatz, *Tikkun Olam* (Aaronson: Northvale, 1997),164. In Orthodox siddurim, i.e. prayer books, a prayer for the welfare of the government, often tailored to the particular country of residence, is recited. It is perhaps an expression of allegiance. It is however, also a reflection of the responsibility stipulated in Jeremiah 29:7.

[2] Jeremiah 29:7.

Amazingly, however, even Reform Judaism now admits that this perspective on social improvements with regards to Tikkun Olam draws heavily from the liberal Protestant tradition of the social gospel. Traditional Jewish attitudes on Tikkun Olam naturally vary throughout rabbinic sources. To what extent Jews should actively engage the world is a complicated question. It is a question whose answer is partly framed by the tragic saga of Jewish history.

Part of this complexity is tied to how traditionally oriented Jews engage the world. In the 21st century, it is easy to lose sight of the historical situation of Jews. In the aftermath of the destruction of the Second Temple near the end of the 1st century CE, a near complete exodus of Jews from the land of Israel occurred. Consequently, Jewish exposure to and confrontation with non-Jewish life and philosophy increased. Jews mainly felt this challenge in the medieval period living in Christian and Islamic civilizations, where Jews often found themselves the primary minority.

There were various ways to deal with this reality. The first approach regarding interaction with the outside world is the so-called Particularistic position which embraces the view that Jewish thinking has its native categories; other modes of non-Jewish thinking are superfluous or even inimical to Jewish thinking and authenticity. It has also been referred to as the "way of insulation" by David Hartman.

At its extreme, the "way of insulation" approach, as Hartman describes, simply rejects and dismisses "foreign modes of thought" by refusing to accept them as serious. Attempting to explain or substantiate Jewish values within the category of another philosophical or religious framework requires the affirmation of the competing system as rational and legitimate to some extent. If one denies outside views as inherently lacking any legitimate claim, then one need only to ignore the claim.[3] The strength and advantage of this position

---

[3] David Hartman, *Maimonides: Torah and Philosophic Quest* (Philadelphia: Jewish Publication Society, 1976), 8.

is its very *insulation* and hence protection of an entire body of knowledge from all severe challenges. Problematic questions are merely denied legitimacy.

The ultimate guarantor of actual knowledge is found in God, as the ultimate source of revelation. With God as the guarantor of real knowledge, any competing claim or loyalty is easily dismissed; moreover, considering alternative foreign claims or philosophies hints of irrationality and arrogance.[4] The act of dedicating oneself to a manner of life decreed by God automatically delegitimizes any claim made by human reason independently made without divine revelation. This view is found in the 12th and 13th centuries in response to the rise of Jewish philosophy but was also espoused by rabbis of the Renaissance period.

For Rabbi Judah Loew of Prague, also known as the *Maharal*, Judaism can only be expressed in its own native terms. For Rabbi Judah Loew, Rabbi Moses ben Maimon, also known as Maimonides or the *Rambam*,

---

[4] Ibid., 9.

poisoned through his exposure to foreign influences since the study of philosophy lent legitimacy to outside knowledge. For the Maharal, truth does not exist outside of Judaism. The Jewish community and the non-Jewish community are very different. That understanding limits Jewish attempts to engage the rest of the world.

There is one agreement between halakhic sources, and that is of the Noachide laws. The seven Noachide laws (or better said the seven categories of Noachide laws) reflect a basic morality which God demands of all humanity. The purpose here is not to in any way, diminish the importance of these much-needed improvements. It is merely to recognize that Tikkun Olam cannot stand on these concepts alone. If history has taught us anything, it is that man has not progressed to higher standards of behavior. On the contrary, man's disposition most often gravitates toward a degenerate state.

The defining characteristic that most Jews consider when they think about this belief is improving and engaging humanity to achieve higher social, moral, and ethical standards. While these issues are indeed crucial to the notion of Tikkun Olam, a critical aspect of it is often lost.[5] The biblical and liturgical traditions, both repositories of Jewish thought and history throughout the centuries, reflect a perspective that may seem somewhat idealistic, archaic or perhaps even ethnocentric in our day and age. They bear out the ideas, however, which ultimately formed the earliest strata of this amorphous concept.

Tikkun Olam ultimately derives and owes its existence to three key components. The first two deal with the physical and spiritual restoration of Israel. The third component and the subject of concern can be best illustrated by the prayer appended to the end of the *Alenu*. The *Al Ken* is among the few sources that explicitly uses a derivative phrase of Tikkun Olam and therefore serves to define this elusive concept best.

"May we soon see Your mighty splendor, to re-move detestable idolatry from the earth, and false gods will be utterly cut off, *to perfect the universe through the Almighty's sovereignty.* Then all humanity will call upon your Name, to turn all of the earth's wicked to You. All the world's inhabitants will recognize and know that to You, and every knee should bend, every tongue should swear...and to the glory of your Name, they will render homage, and they will all accept upon themselves the yoke of Your King-ship that you may reign over them soon and eternally..."[6]

The *Al Ken* longs for the day that Israel may see God's splendor in the removal of idolatry from the earth as the Hebrew states,

---

[6] Nosson Scherman,*The Complete Artscroll Nusach Ashkenaz* (Brooklyn: Mesorah Publications, 2005), 161.

"taken olam b'malchut sh'dai - to perfect the universe through the Almighty's sovereignty."

The perfecting or improving the world centers on the adulation of God as king over all the earth through the elimination of idolatry. The longing for all humanity to serve God is a theme, which is also affirmed, in various eschatologically minded prayers in the liturgy for the holidays of Rosh Hashanah (Jewish New Year/Day of Judgment) and Succot (Festival of Booths). During the Mussaf service for Shabbat on the first day of Rosh Hashanah, the following prayer is recited during the Musaf Amidah before the sectioned titled Hayom Ha-rat:

"Our God and the God of our forefathers, reign over the entire universe in Your glory; be exalted over all the world in Your splendor, reveal Yourself In the majestic grandeur of Your strength over all the dwellers of Your inhabited world. Let everything that has been made know that you are its Maker...and ...proclaim' Hashem, the God of Israel, is King and His kingship rules over everything."[7]

In the Hoshiah prayers from the Hoshanah Rabbah liturgy, we read,

"Save your people and bless Your heritage, tend them and elevate them forever. May these words of mine, which I have supplicated before Hashem, be near to Hashem, our God, by day and by night; that He bring about justice for His servant and justice for His people, Israel, each day's need in its day; that all the people of the earth shall know that Hashem is God and there is no other."[8]

---

[7] Nosson Scherman, *The Complete Arscroll Machzor-Rosh Hashanah Nusach Sefard* (Mesorah Publications, 2000), 453.

[8] Nosson Scherman, *The Complete Arscroll Machzor-Succot Nusach Ashkenaz* (Mesorah Publications, 1997), 739.

Restoration, according to these prayers, requires the elimination of idolatry, the "enthronement" and the dissemination of the knowledge of God as king over all the earth and its inhabitants. The *Y'Hi Chavod* in the Shacharit for Shabbat states that,

"...the heavens will be glad, and the earth will rejoice, they will proclaim among the nations.' Hashem has reigned!' Hashem reigns, Hashem has reigned. Hashem will reign for all eternity."[9]

The prophet Isaiah also relates:

"And it shall come to pass at the end of days, that the mountain of the LORD'S house shall be established as the top of the mountains, and shall be exalted above the hills; and all nations shall flow unto it.

---

[9] Nosson Scherman, *The Complete Arscroll Machzor-Succot Nusach Ashkenaz* (Mesorah Publications, 1997), 67.

And many peoples shall go and say: 'Come ye, and let us go up to the mountain of the LORD, to the house of the God of Jacob; and He will teach us of His ways, and we will walk in His paths.' For out of Zion shall go forth the law, and the word of the LORD from Jerusalem."[10]

The prophet Isaiah continues with the following declaration.

"For I [know] their works and their thoughts; [the time] cometh, that I will gather all nations and tongues; and *they shall come, and shall see My glory.*"[11]

The ultimate goal of Tikkun Olam then is to restore and return both Israel and humanity to the primeval knowledge of God as experienced initially in the

---

[10] Isaiah 2:2-3.
[11] Isaiah 66:18.

creation and Gan Eden, i.e., the Garden of Eden.[12] It might be asked how such lofty goals are to be achieved. Was or is God expected to miraculously reveal himself to every nation as he did to Israel? Alternatively, does B'nai Israel, i.e., the children of Israel, form an integral part of God's view of Tikkun Olam? [13] This is the subject of the next chapter.

---

[12] Rabbi Abba bar Kahana said: "Originally the Shekhinah was in the earthly world, [but] when Adam sinned, the Shekhinah retreated to the lowermost heaven." (BR 19:7). *The Ariel Chumash* (Jerusalem: Ariel: 1997), 69.

[13] There are several Midrashim that allude to the idea that in the past God did reveal Himself to the nations, but they rejected His advances towards them. "The Torah was given in public, for all to see, in the open. For if it had been given in the Land of Israel, Israel would have said to the nations of the world, You have no share in it; Therefore the Torah was given in the wilderness, in public, for all to see, in the open, and everyone who wishes to receive it, let him come and receive it." Mechilta 15:26.

CHAPTER 2

The History of Israel Speaks to the World

The actual knowledge of God is spread among humanity, ultimately by God himself, *though* Israel's ongoing history serves as the medium. The portion of the Shacharit (morning) service titled *Pesukei d'Zimrah* or the morning songs of praise includes a passage from the book of Chronicles. The Chronicler declares that Israel should,

"…Proclaim his deeds among the people…"

The passage continues with a charge to Israel to recall God's wonders by communicating His glory among the nations. God's covenant with the Patriarchs is recounted and as well as God's deliverance for the people of Israel in the wilderness. The Chronicler proclaims,

"...great is the Lord and exalted in praise, yea he is awesome of above all gods, for all the gods of the heathen are idols."[1]

The Chronicler culminates with adulation and praise concerning God's majestic nature and subsequently calls upon the nations to abandon idolatry and to render homage, glory, and a *mincha* offering to the one true God.

Psalm 67, recited by many congregations as a preliminary prayer for the Maariv, i.e., the evening service on Shabbat, confirms the view that God's desire for perfecting the world includes at its core, an expectation that Israel will serve to *save* or illuminate humanity to monotheism.

---

[1] See I Chronicles 16: 8-36. See David de Sola Pool, *Book of Prayers: According to the Custom of the Spanish and Portuguese Jews* (New York: Union of Sephardic Congregations, 2001), 19-20.

"For the Conductor, upon Neginos, a psalm a song, May God favor us and bless us, may He illuminate His countenance with us. Selah. To make known Your way on the earth, among all the nations Your salvation. The peoples will acknowledge you o God, the peoples will acknowledge You, O God, all of them. Nations will be glad and sing for joy, because You will judge the peoples fairly and guide the nations of the earth, Selah. The peoples will acknowledge You, O God, the peoples will acknowledge You, all of them. The earth has yielded produce, may God, our own God, bless us. May God bless us and may all the ends of the earth fear Him."[2]

The argument in Jewish thought has centered on the question of how much if, any Jewish participation in teaching or accountability for Gentile violations of the Noachide laws exists. Rabbi Moses ben Maimon, also known as the *Rambam,* took what appears to be the

---

[2] Psalm 67.

minority position among the Sages that Jews, as well as Gentiles, are indeed responsible for ensuring that the Noachic laws are observed to the best of their ability. This position though not necessarily corroborated explicitly within liturgical sources, does find considerable support throughout the siddur, in my opinion.

The majority position espoused by later authorities such as Rabbi Moses Isserles, also known as the *Rama*, rejected this view on the premise that no such halakhic obligation existed.

The majority of the sages maintained a position that required Jews to be ready to respond to the inquiries of interested Gentiles concerning what laws apply to them and how best to observe them. While Jewish history points out the limited role especially in post-Temple times that Jews can play in perfecting the world, the siddur ultimately holds out the expectation that Jews will draw the nations to the knowledge of God.

In Psalm 67, Israel asks God for favor and blessing that it may, make known,

"Your way on earth, among all the nations Your salvation."

It is quite clear then that the Psalmist expected God's blessing upon Jews to serve beyond any self-serving purpose. If Jews observed the mitzvoth, i.e., the commandments, as revealed at Sinai, as the *Kriat Shema* reveals, God would be sure to provide for Jews without restraint. Furthermore, the nations would stand in awe of Israel's Torah and turn to Israel's God. The *Kriat Shema* makes it clear that Israel obedience of Torah would ensue with a great reward. The second paragraph states:

"And it will come to pass that if you continually hearken to My commandments that I command you today, to love Hashem, your God, and to serve Him, with all of your heart and with all of your soul- then I will provide rain for you land in its proper time, the early and late rains, that you may gather in your grain, you wine and your oil,

I will provide grass for field for your cattle and you will eat and be satisfied." [3]

The prophetic tradition in Judaism bears witness to the fact that the children of Israel have not always walked faithfully by the Torah. Amazingly, however, even Israel's punishment and seemingly unending tragedies do not preclude the goal of Tikkun Olam from being realized. Israel's repentance eventually leads not only to restoration for its sins but also catalyzes the nations to acknowledge God's hand in history.

In Israel's punishment, the nations would see God's judgment. In Israel's restoration, they would also see God's mercy. As a consequence, they would recognize God's intervention, mercy, and power. Psalm 126 (*Shir Hamalot*) recited at the commencement of *Bircat Hamazon* (Grace after Meals) reflects this idea that the nations will understand the hand of God in Israel's historical and ongoing redemption.

---

[3] Deuteronomy 11:14. Nosson Scherman,*The Complete Artscroll Nusach Ashkenaz* (Brooklyn: Mesorah Publications, 2005), 93.

"When Hashem will return the captivity of Zion, we will be like dreamers…Then they will declare among the nations 'Hashem has done greatly with these.'"[4]

In the same manner, the prayers titled the *Tahanut L'Shacharit* (penitential prayers) according to the Spanish-Portuguese tradition further illustrate this insight by appealing to God for redemption from the four corners of the earth.

"Our Father, merciful Father, show us a token of good and gather our dispersed from the four corners of the whole earth. Then shall all the nations know and acknowledge that Thou Lord art our Father."[5]

---

[4] Nosson Scherman,*The Complete Artscroll Nusach Ashkenaz* (Brooklyn: Mesorah Publications, 2005), 183.

[5] David de Sola Pool, *Book of Prayers: According to the Custom of the Spanish and Portuguese Jews*

The nations seeing the restoration of Israel would consequently acknowledge the unique creator.

Biblical and Liturgical Perspectives of Tikkun Olam

Amazingly the siddur not only contains passages which openly support the view that Tikkun Olam centers on directing humanity to God, but it also includes a series of readings that serve to elaborate on Tikkun Olam. It does so by recalling and revealing God's desire of recreating and replicating a Gan Eden like experience in each of God's redemptive acts for Israel.

As we saw, I Chronicles sets the stage for Israel to proclaim God's glory among the nations by recounting His splendid and redemptive works. Jewish liturgy bears witness to these fundamental concepts by appealing to several recurring themes. Among them are God's involvement and sovereignty in creation and Is-

(New York. Union of Sephardic Congregations, 2001), 75.

rael's redemption from Egypt and encounter with God at Sinai.

The second group of these events we might suggest is a replica, as we shall hope to see in the first event. Each theme, however, is inevitably linked to the previous concept. Each act of deliverance or redemption recalls the past and attempts to establish or re-establish the prior state of spiritual and physical existence.

God's Redemptive Acts among the Nations

God's deliverance of Israel from Egypt serves to illustrate further the goal of perfecting and restoring the world through the knowledge of God. The Exodus from Egypt had two noticeable purposes. The first purpose was to create a people that have experienced bondage and servitude, as well as ultimate redemption, would understand God's love for them fully through His miraculous deliverance.

There is a second purpose, however, which is often overlooked. Israel's deliverance from Egypt strikes at the heart of Tikkun Olam as we saw in the *Al Ken*. It was to demonstrate to Egypt the supremacy and nature of God above and over the gods of Egypt. The book of Exodus informs us that God hardened the heart of Pharaoh with an ulterior motive:

> "But I will harden Pharaoh's heart, *that I may multiply my signs and marvels in the Land of Egypt… And the Egyptians shall know that I am the Lord* when I stretch out my hand over Egypt and bring out the Israelites from their midst."[6]

When the armies of Israel under Joshua began the conquest of the land of Canaan, the Canaanite nations responded with fear to Israel's eventful history.

> "For we have heard how the Lord dried up the waters of the Sea of Reeds for you when you left Egypt…When we heard about it, we lost

---

[6] Exodus 7:4-6.

heart…for the Lord your God is the only God in heaven above and on earth below."[7]

It would seem, therefore, that God's deliverance for Israel ultimately caused the nations of Canaan to confront the Divine reality. God had acted deliberately in creation on behalf of his chosen people. The Genesis accounts of God's sovereignty were being played out before the nations, as we shall see. The history of Israel reveals the stage on which the existence of God and his image-bearing into creation is made manifest. The prayer book contains various passages that serve to remind Jews daily of the redemption from Egypt. [8]

---

[7] Joshua 2:10-11.

[8] See *Vayomer Adonai* (Numbers 15: 37-41) as part of the Kriat Shema; Daniel 9: 15-19. David de Sola Pool, *Book of Prayers: According to the Custom of the Spanish and Portuguese Jews* (New York. Union of Sephardic Congregations, 2001). See also Mi Kamocha/ Nora Tehilot, preceding the Shemoneh Esreh; Kiddush.

The Perfection which Tikkun Olam Aims

As we mentioned earlier, the siddur highlights several recurring themes. Creation and God's creative role in history is stressed.

"Ere Thy world's creation One thou wast; since creation Thou wast; since creation Thou art One. God Thou art in this world; Thou wilt be God in the world to come. …Sanctify Thy name in this Thy world through Israel, a people hallowing Thy name…Blessed the one who hallows Thy name before mankind!"[9]

God's miraculous power and his uniqueness are acknowledged in the recitation of the HaMeir which follows the Yotzer Ohr:

---

[9] David de Sola Pool, *Book of Prayers: According to the Custom of the Spanish and Portuguese Jews* (New York. Union of Sephardic Congregations, 2001), 9.

"He creates light ... and renews daily, perpetually the work of creation..."[10]

Genesis bears out God's sovereignty over nature, a vital component of the liturgical tradition. It relates, more importantly, God's initial engagement with man, in an ideal state free from the constant physical and spiritual distractions, i.e., perhaps a greater preponderance toward the Yetzer Hara we encounter today. The *Adon Olam* states,

"The King who was exalted in Solitude,"

not only created but connected with man, the chief of his creation without constraint or barrier.

Amazingly, Adam alone-received God's spirit amidst the grandeur of an array of celestial bodies that far exceeded that of any one person. This type of spir-

---

[10] Nosson Scherman,*The Complete Artscroll Nusach Ashkenaz* (Brooklyn: Mesorah Publications, 2005), 85-86.

itual connectedness or an intimacy even remotely approaching this is indeed rare in the biblical tradition. Personages such as Enoch, Abraham, and Moses are among the few individuals who could recreate even an aspect of Gan Eden.

They approached the creator in a manner that resembled and recreated what one might argue to be the perfect ideal reflected in Gan Eden. The Hebrew Scripture records of Moses that he talked with God as a man speaks to his friend. God's engagement with man in the garden reflected an intermediary state between the world of the Divine and the world, as we know it today. Indeed, it can be argued that the picture of Israel's history portrays God attempt to mimic or recreate his acts of creation reflective of Israel's desire to return to previous days.[11]

---

[11] "Bring us back to You Hashem and we shall return, renew our days as of old." Etz Chaim following the Completion of the Torah Service. Nosson Scherman,*The Complete Artscroll Nusach Ashkenaz* (Brooklyn: Mesorah Publications, 2005), 461.

Gan Eden and Universal Knowledge of God

The Blessings of the Shema for Shabbat relate that the angels stand at the summit of the universe ready to proclaim their reverence for God's name.[12] These angels proclaim the holiness of God.

The Hebrew term for holiness is *Kedushah*. In actuality, it communicates the concept of separation and distance from God's relationship with creation. God's, as the *Kedushah* reflects is,

"Holy, Holy, Holy"
"Kadosh, Kadosh, Kadosh."

---

[12] From the *Titbarach/Et Shem*, "…all of Whose ministering angels stand at the summit of the universe and proclaim with awe…Holy, Holy, Holy is Hashem, Master of Legions, the whole world is filled with His glory." Nosson Scherman,*The Complete Artscroll Nusach Ashkenaz* (Brooklyn: Mesorah Publications, 2005), 413.

He is ultimately separated from what creation can perceive or understand. Subsequently, Jewish liturgy communicates the challenge of humanity's encounter to engage the Divine, the Ineffable tangibly. In our day and age, what can we hope to learn of God? It is often asked how we communicate with what may seem un-reachable or un-penetrable?

Gan Eden is the answer or better said the goal at which Tikkun Olam aims. In Gan Eden, man stood at the center of God's creation. His interaction with God, most importantly, was close and personal, physically and spiritually. Gan Eden sheds light on one more critical aspect. All "men" knew and served the creator. All acknowledged God's kingship. No other alternative was possible.

Regardless of Adam's sin, God's sole existence as both King and Creator was not open to question. Unfortunately, as time passed, humanity found other forms to acknowledge as creator and as divine. Genesis relates to us the story of Noah and the great Deluge, a point in history at which humanity became worshippers of graven idols. This refers to the theme we saw earlier in the *Al Ken* concerning idolatry among the nations.

Adam's subsequent fall and humanity's gradual decadence had dire consequences, however. The Divine presence or the Shechinah to some extent was removed much in a manner that closely resembles the way that the Shechinah was removed from Eretz Israel at the destruction of the First Temple.[13] Though God remained involved in the creation, the physical components of His presence were now not so readily perceived.

---

[13] *V'te'hezenah* in the weekday Amidah reads "May our eyes behold Your return to Zion in compassion. Blessed are you, Hashem who restores His presence to Zion." Nosson Scherman, *The Complete Artscroll Nusach Ashkenaz* (Brooklyn: Mesorah Publications, 2005), 111.

CHAPTER 3

Abraham Encounters God

God's interaction with Abraham and then with Israel opens a new chapter in human history. Abraham was called out of the land of Ur, out of idolatry.[1] Concerning Abraham, Rabbi Samson Raphael Hirsch commented,

"When in the choice of Abraham, the foundation of this people was laid, God. Who did it, pronounced its significance: 'and in you shall all families of the earth be blessed.'...For I know him, that he will command his children and his household after him, and they shall keep the way of the Lord, to do justice and judgment." [Gen

---

[1] Genesis 12.

18:18]...As the priest among the people, so should they among humanity uphold the vision of God and humanity and by so doing be a holy nation, raised above every injustice, profaneness, and hard-heartedness, as becomes the bearers of such a message...that the whole of humanity, awakened by its own experience, enlightened anew and uplifted by our destiny and life, should, in unity with us, turn to the One and Only- and *if thus we would fulfill our vocation as priests to humanity* – what bliss there would be..."[2]

From this point forward, God's involvement in history through the children of Israel strives for one purpose, a return to the primeval relationship between Creator and creation. While Genesis records the cause of creation, Exodus, in turn, records the ultimate purpose or cause of creation.

According to Rabbi Solomon ben Isaac, who was also known as *Rashi*, the world was created on account

---

[2] Horeb, no. 613.

of "*reshit*," "on behalf of Israel, which is termed re-shit." Rabbi Naphtali Zevi Yehudah Berlin relates that the purpose of creation was not fulfilled until Israel exited from Egypt and achieved their end purpose in illuminating the nations and causing them to arrive at the knowledge of the God of creation.[3]

Abraham's search for God eventually leads to binding of Isaac, the *Akedah*, which is, recited daily in the morning Shacharit. It concludes with the familiar phrase rewarding Abraham's unmitigated fidelity to God,

"I shall surely bless you … and all the nations shall bless themselves by your offspring because you have listened to my voice."[4]

It is also written in Genesis that through Abraham, all the nations would be blessed. What blessing could

---

[3] David Shatz, *Tikkun Olam* (Aaronson: Northvale, 1997), 89.

[4] Genesis 22:17-19.

cause the nations to praise Abraham and his descendants?

The *Shema V'ahavta* perhaps provides a clue. The cornerstone of Jewish faith reads,

> "And you shall love the Lord your God...
> *V'ahavta et Adonai Elokekha*."

How does the Shema inform us concerning Abraham's gift to the world? Hazal's commentary on this passage rereads "Vahavta" as "Ahavehu." Instead of

> "And you shall love the Lord."

the new reading renders this phrase as

> "And you *shall make* Him *beloved*."

Abraham and Sarah's role in spreading the knowledge of God is well known in Midrash.[5] For example, Abra-

---

[5] Midrash Tanhuma, Lekh Lekha 12.

ham and Sarah fed hungry travelers and then directed their gratefulness to God, the ultimate provider of humanity. Abraham reconnected men with the real God; a small yet pertinent glimpse of the connectedness present in Gan Eden.

The Parting of the Red Sea

The retelling of God's miracles in the creation and its interconnectedness to both the Exodus and Shabbat is another crucial topic found in the siddur. The Hakol Yoducha conveys God's uniqueness as the architect of creation:

> "…You who forms everything. The God who opens daily the doors of the gateways of the East, and splits the windows of the firmament, who removes the sun from its place and the moon

from the site of its dwelling, and who illuminates all the work and its inhabitants...”[6]

Israel attempts to proclaim man's engagement of the Divine and relate his greatness. It does not take too much effort for us to realize that God's creative acts are well noted throughout the siddur. The *Birchot haShachar*, i.e., the morning blessings, portrays in miniature God's creative acts as recorded in Genesis. In Genesis, God created the heavens and the earth. The morning blessings proclaim daily God's role as creator, the manipulator, and master over nature:

"Thou art the Lord God in all of the spheres of heaven above and on the earth beneath. ...Thou hast made the heavens, the earth, the sea, and all that is in them. Who among all the works of Thy

---

[6] Nosson Scherman,*The Complete Artscroll Nusach Ashkenaz* (Brooklyn: Mesorah Publications, 2005), 409.

hands, celestial or terrestrial, can say unto thee, "What does Thou, what workest Thou?"[7]

The Song at the Sea

We mentioned previously that a partial acting out of Tikkun Olam's goal might be seen in the redemption of Israel from Egypt. Now we will examine the miracle at the Sea of Reeds and parallel this with God's role as creator in Genesis. The splitting of the Red Sea, Israel's encounter with God at Sinai and Israel's eventual entry to the land, parallels God creative acts in Genesis. In Genesis, God created light and darkness.

He created the heavens by separating the waters from the waters. He made dry land appear and placed man in the Gan Eden where He revealed his Presence to man. There as we noted previously, He interacted with man. God's creative acts are seen in three key ar-

---

[7] David de Sola Pool, *Book of Prayers: According to the Custom of the Spanish and Portuguese Jews* (New York. Union of Se-phardic Congregations, 2001), 9.

eas: his mastery over the celestial bodies, His mastery over the waters, and His mastery over the earth and its produce. These actions are mirrored in God's deliverance of Israel from Egypt.

At the Sea of Reeds, Tikkun Olam was being worked out by God. God intervened on Israel's behalf by replicating his creative acts in Genesis. Exodus 14:19 informs us that the angel of the Lord caused a separation to occur between the Israelites and the pursuing Egyptians. What follows is a re-creation of the Genesis account.

> "The angel of God, who had been going ahead of the Israelite army, now moved and followed behind them; and the pillar of cloud shifted from in front of them and took up a place behind them, and it came between the army of the Egyptians and the army of Israel."[8]

---

[8] Exodus 14:19.

The pillar of cloud acting as God's emissary or agent, caused darkness to surround the Egyptians while the pillar of fire provided light for the Israelites fleeing. The similarity between the pillar of cloud hovering over Israel and the Divine presence hovering over the waters in Genesis 1:1 is striking given the description found in Hazal's commentary concerning the Shechinah hovering over the waters as depicted in Genesis. According to the Hazal, within the cloud of glory stood the throne of God. As in Genesis, God separated[9] the light from the darkness.[10] The account continues with

---

[9] The separation of the two camps by means of darkness and light reflects what the sages note about creation. Darkness is not merely the absence of light, but a specific creation, as is clearly stated in Isaiah 45:7, "He forms the light and creates darkness."

[10] "On this night, the cloud (pillar) was placed between the Jews and the Egyptians, where it served a dual purpose. It prevented the Egyptians from benefiting from the illumination of the pillar of light, thus plunging them into total darkness. Meanwhile, the pillar of cloud, though not specifically mentioned in the verse, illuminated the night for Israel (Rashi). Nosson Scherman, *The Chumash-Nusach Sefard* (Brooklyn: Mesorah Publications, 2001), 372.

Moses' supplication to God concerning the next step to take. At God's behest, Moses stretches out his hand over the waters and

> "The LORD moved the sea with a strong east wind all night...The children of Israel came within the sea on dry land, and the water was a wall for them on their right hand and their left."[11]

Once again, this parallels the Genesis account. The waters were separated, and dry land was made to appear. If we agree to the similarity of these events, then the logical correlation between Gan Eden is Israel's journey to Sinai to meet God, "face to face" just as Adam did.

The *Yashir Moshe*, the song of Moses at the Sea of Reeds, sung during the Shacharit service on Shabbat, recounts these events.

---

[11] Exodus 14:21-22.

"Israel saw the great hand that Hashem inflicted upon Egypt, and the people feared Hashem, and they had faith in Hashem and in Moses, his servant...You shall bring them and implant them on the mount of your heritage, the foundation of Your dwelling place, which you Hashem, have made: the Sanctuary, my Lord, that your hands established...For the sovereignty is Hashem's and He rules over the nations...Then Hashem will be King over all the world, on that day Hashem will be one, and His name will be One."[12]

Shabbat as a Memorial of the Exodus and Creation

We should remember that the critical aspect of Gan Eden was man's encounter with God and the intimate dialogue that occurred between them. Shabbat, as the

---

[12] Nosson Scherman, *The Complete Artscroll Nusach Ashkenaz* (Brooklyn: Mesorah Publications, 2005), 399-401.

Torah relates, is a sign of God's Sinaitic covenant with Israel. We have sought to argue that Tikkun Olam aims to recreate creation concerning the knowledge of God. Subsequently, Israel relates God's uniqueness by recounting its history. Central to Israel's history and identity is the Shabbat. Indeed as the *V'shamru* states, Shabbat is Israel's covenantal sign with God.

"…The Children of Israel shall keep the Sabbath, to make the Sabbath an eternal covenant for their generations. Between Me and the Children of Israel, it is a sign forever that in six days Hashem made heaven and earth, and on the seventh day He rested and was refreshed…"[13]

The Kiddush for Shabbat Evening continues this by calling Israel to remember God's wondrous works. If the redemption at the Sea of Reeds replicated God's miracles at Creation, then Sinai replicates the height of

Gan Eden. However, Shabbat does not merely serve as a reminder of God's intimacy with Israel.

Amid a world, which denies the existence or supremacy of Hashem, Shabbat served as the primary tool by which Israel might boldly proclaim the revelation of God to humanity. To observe Shabbat is to announce the sanctity of both the Creator and the creation. Shabbat not only serves to remind the children of Israel of God's encounter with them at Sinai but as a memory of creation.

The Kabbalat Shabbat service is primarily composed of several Psalms welcoming the onset of the Sabbath. It was initially formulated with the view that Shabbat was to be likened to a queen that brought majesty into the midst of her subjects. Even in their anticipation of Shabbat, several of these Psalms continue to relate the idea that Israel must communicate God's glory among the nations. Psalm 96 proclaims,

"Relate His Glory among the nations, among all peoples, His wonders; that Hashem is great and exceedingly lauded... for all of the gods of the nations are nothing- but Hashem made heaven!"[14]

Psalm 97 continues this idea with a longing for God's kingdom on earth to be established:

"When Hashem will reign, the world will rejoice numerous islands will be glad. ...And all the people will see His glory..."[15]

However, the nations will not only see they will also gratefully praise God.

"When Hashem will reign nations will tremble...They will gratefully praise Your great and awesome Name."[16]

---

[14] Psalm 96:3, 5.
[15] Psalm 97:1, 6.
[16] Psalm 99.

From the Kabbalat Shabbat we turn to the prelude for *Kiddush l'Shabbat* where it states:

"The sixth day. Thus the heavens and the earth were finished, and all their array. On the seventh day from all His work which He had done. God blessed the seventh day and hallowed it because on it He abstained from all His work which God created to make...Blessed are You, Hashem our God, King of the Universe, who has sanctified us with His commandments, took pleasure in us, and with love and favor gave us His Holy Sabbath as a heritage, a remembrance of creation..."[17]

Shabbat also serves as another model, which Tikkun Olam seeks to recreate. Shabbat is an island of rest, or-

---

[17] Nosson Scherman,*The Complete Artscroll Nusach Ashkenaz* (Brooklyn: Mesorah Publications, 2005), 365.

der and restoration.[18] Shabbat must be understood as a picture of both spiritual bliss and peace which echoes God's original creation.

Israel's observance of Shabbat proclaims to the nations that the King of the universe contracted and covenanted with a people to relate his desire to fellowship with all humanity. Israel's history bears out this divine exchange between humanity and the struggle to know and sense who He is.

The Spread of God's Knowledge

Rabbi Moses ben Maimon relates the idea that even the existence of religious groups which have at times persecuted Jews are part of the spread of God's

---

[18] Mishnah Tamid 7:4 (Mussaf for Shabbat) The daily that the Levites would recite in the Temple was as follows: "On the Sabbath Day they would say: A psalm, a song for the time to come, to the day that will be entirely Sabbath and contentment for the eternal life."

knowledge among the nations. Regarding the activities of Christianity and Islam, the Rambam states they are:

"…all for the purpose of paving the way for the true King Messiah, and preparing the entire world to worship God together, as is written (Tzefaniah 3,9): 'For then I will convert the nations to a pure language, that they may all call in the name of God and serve Him together.'

How will this work? For by then, the world will already be filled with the idea of Messiah, and Torah, and commandments, even in far-off islands and in closed-hearted nations, where they engage in discussions on the Torah"s commandments: some say that the Torah's commandments are true but are no longer binding in these times, while others say that there are hidden, deep meanings to them, and that the Messiah has come and revealed their hidden secrets. But when the true King Messiah arrives, and will succeed and will raise them up, all the peoples will immediately realize that they had been taught lies by their forefathers, and that their ancestors and prophets had misled them."[19]

In a much later work, Rabbi Judah Assael del Bene of Ferrara in the 17th century relates the following perspective regarding Christian missionaries in his day.

"Even if they do not observe the words of this Torah as we do today, nevertheless, they still believe that it is the Torah from heaven that was given at Sinai by Moses...for it was God's holy will to awaken a spirit of men of very good virtues, masters of a language spoken according to the Torah today who are called Christian to spread out afar a fence to those distant islands and to succeed in their purpose.[20]

---

[19] Mishneh Torah Hilchot Melachim 11, 4.

[20] David R. Ruderman, *Jewish Thought and Scientific Discovery in Early Modern Europe* (Detroit: Wayne State University, 1995), 195.

Conclusion

Tikkun Olam is indeed a complicated subject. It certainly includes the idea of a Godly partnership with humanity to make the world a better place. Jews and Judaism indeed bear this responsibility.

All branches of Judaism most readily agree upon human responsibility before God and his fellow man to live ethical and moral lives. Indeed, Jews are charged with engaging humanity to reach higher standards.

Nevertheless, modern society has invariably influenced Jewish thought concerning long-held theological positions, including Tikkun Olam. However, the ultimate goal of spreading the knowledge of the God of Israel as both king and the creator must remain a central piece in Israel's mission as a light unto the nations. Jewish identity must have a purpose beyond self-preservation. It must be the vehicle through which the God of Israel is known throughout the earth.

Bibliography

The Ariel Institute. The Ariel Chumash. Jerusalem: Ariel. 1997.

David Hartman, *Maimonides: Torah and Philosophic Quest.* Philadelphia: Jewish Publication Society, 1976.

David R. Ruderman. *Jewish Thought and Scientific Discovery in Early Modern Europe.* Detroit: Wayne State University. 1995.

Nosson Scherman. *The Chumash-Nusach Sefard.* Brooklyn: Mesorah Publications, 2001.

Nosson Scherman. *The Complete Artscroll Nusach Ashkenaz.* Brooklyn: Mesorah Publications, 2005.

Nosson Scherman. *The Complete Artscroll Machzor-Rosh Hashanah Nusach Sefard.* Mesorah Publications. 2000.

Nosson Scherman. *The Complete Artscroll Machzor-Succot Nusach Ashkenaz.* Mesorah Publications, 1997.

David Shatz. *Tikkun Olam.* Aaronson: Northvale, 1997.

David de Sola Pool. Book of Prayers: According to the Custom of the Spanish and Portuguese Jews. New York. Union of Sephardic Congregations. 2001.

Backlist Titles

Juan Marcos Bejarano Gutierrez *What is Jewish Prayer?*Yaron Publishing. 2016.

Juan Marcos Bejarano Gutierrez. *Who is a Jew?* Yaron Publishing. 2016.

Juan Marcos Bejarano Gutierrez. *What is Jewish Prayer?* Yaron Publishing. 2016.

Juan Marcos Bejarano Gutierrez. *Against the Greeks: Understanding the Classical Jewish Worldview.* Yaron Publishing. 2017.

Juan Marcos Bejarano Gutierrez *Secret Jews: The Complex Identity of Crypto-Jews and Crypto-Judaism.* Yaron Publishing. 2016

Juan Marcos Bejarano Gutierrez *The Rise of the Inquisition: An Introduction to the Spanish and Portuguese Inquisitions.*Yaron Publishing. 2016

Index

ABOUT THE AUTHOR

Juan Marcos Bejarano Gutierrez is a graduate of the University of Texas at Dallas where he earned a bachelor of science in electrical engineering. He works full time as an engineer but has devoted much of his time to Jewish studies. He studied at the Siegal College of Judaic Studies in Cleveland and received a Master of Arts Degree in Judaic Studies. He completed his doctoral studies at the Spertus Institute in Chicago in 2015. He studied at the American Seminary for Contemporary Judaism and received rabbinic ordination in 2011 from Yeshiva Mesilat Yesharim.

Juan Marcos Bejarano Gutierrez was a board member of the Society for Crypto-Judaic Studies from 2011-2013. He has published various articles in HaLapid, The Journal for Spanish, Portuguese, and Italian Crypto-Jews, and Apuntes-Theological Reflections from a Hispanic-Latino Context, and is the author of *What is Kosher?* and *What is Jewish Prayer?* and *Secret Jews: The Complex Identity of Crypto-Jews and Crypto-Judaism*. He is currently the director of the B'nai Anusim Center for Education at CryptoJewishEducation.com which provides additional information on the Inquisition as well as the phenomena of Crypto-Judaism.

If you have enjoyed this book or others that are part of this series, please consider leaving a positive review on Amazon or Goodreads. A positive review helps spread the word about this book and encourages others to study and learn something new.

Made in the USA
Las Vegas, NV
30 July 2021